Waiting Without Worrying

Choosing Hope in the Unbearable

Mackenzie Kambizi

Copyright © 2020 by **Mackenzie Kambizi**

All rights reserved. No part of this publication may be reproduced, distributed, or transmitted in any form or by any means, without prior written permission.

Scripture quotations marked (ESV) are taken from the ESV® Bible (The Holy Bible, English Standard Version®). ESV® Text Edition: 2016. Copyright © 2001 by Crossway, a publishing ministry of Good News Publishers. The ESV® text has been reproduced in cooperation with and by permission of Good News Publishers. Unauthorized reproduction of this publication is prohibited. Used by permission. All rights reserved.

Scripture quotations marked (NIV) are taken from the Holy Bible, New International Version®, NIV® Copyright © 1973, 1978, 1984, 2011 by Biblica, Inc.® Used by permission. All rights reserved worldwide.

Scripture quotations marked (NKJV) are taken from the New King James Version®. Copyright © 1982 by Thomas Nelson, Inc. Used by permission. All rights reserved.

Renown Publishing
www.renownpublishing.com

Waiting Without Worrying / Mackenzie Kambizi
ISBN-13: 978-1-952602-14-6

For Chamu—a good man gone too soon. You are a young brother any big brother would desire to have. You are a friend I always needed, a confidant I trusted, and my anchor in support. You changed my life the day you were born, and you did it again the day you passed away. I am going to be waiting without worrying till I see you again soon, when Jesus appears. Rest in hope, my Champ—rest on!

For my elegant children—Madison, Morgan, Unathi, and Nkosi-Mackenzie-Chamu Jr.

And for all who have had the opportunity and privilege of waiting in the unbearable!

CONTENTS

Waiting As a Christian 3
When It's Been Too Long 7
Jesus Will Never Leave You 21
Servants in Training 35
Knowing God's Divinity 47
When Blessings Delay 57
A Willing Participant 69
Waiting in the Unbearable 81
Thriving in the Unbearable 93
Bust a Move 105
About the Author 113
Notes 115

INTRODUCTION

Waiting As a Christian

There are two kinds of waiting: when you're looking forward to something good or when you're dreading something awful. The good kind of waiting makes time drag so slowly that you think the earth has stopped. For example, Christmas can't come soon enough because the package beside the tree is shaped just like the bike you've always wanted. Why your parents wrapped it is anyone's guess, but there it is. You're dreaming about the wheels rolling below you, the freedom, the speed, and the wind in your hair. Waiting is so hard, yet also pleasurable and exhilarating.

The bad kind of waiting is knowing that there's a difficult surgery coming up and it's going to hurt. It will be a difficult recovery, and you must wait for news on the biopsy. Waiting is so hard, and in these instances, you need the power of God. That is the kind of waiting this book addresses.

We will focus on three words: *waiting without worrying*. You may often worry as you wait, but is it possible to wait without worrying? Think about it.

Most human beings can agree that waiting is hard. It is a challenge no matter how close you are to God. Just sitting in the waiting room at your doctor's office for a routine checkup is enough to make you fidget. And what about the airport? You're ready to fly, but the plane is not there yet or they need to clean it, and you're going to be late. What about being the groom on your wedding day? You stand at the altar and wait for your bride while every story you've ever heard about brides changing their minds plays through your head. You are dying inside, hoping that she'll show up.

Waiting is a difficult aspect of the human life, but God doesn't ask you to wait without help or encouragement. What does the Bible say about waiting?

1. Waiting brings *change*.
2. Waiting demands a *choice*.
3. Waiting presents a *challenge*.

The Three Cs of Waiting

Whenever you wait for something to *change, choice* and *challenge* occur, in that order. If you're prepared to deal with each of these, worry doesn't enter the equation.

The future is uncertain, and it requires waiting. In turn, waiting produces a change in you because it requires a choice. Waiting will present a challenge for you if worry is your natural emotional response. Why? Because you're unprepared.

In the following chapters, you will learn that faith in the Lord and hope in His Word will produce a blessing of waiting without worrying as you trust His divine will for your life. Moreover, a workbook section at the end of each chapter will help you to change, to choose, and to overcome your challenges.

Proverbs 8:34 states, "Blessed are those who listen to

me, watching daily at my doors, waiting at my doorway" (NIV). This book was written to prepare you for your season of waiting. As you wait, do so with the confidence and trust that your Heavenly Father is right alongside you to equip you and to strengthen you.

CHAPTER ONE

When It's Been Too Long

Some time later, Jesus went up to Jerusalem for one of the Jewish festivals. Now there is in Jerusalem near the Sheep Gate a pool, which in Aramaic is called Bethesda and which is surrounded by five covered colonnades. Here a great number of disabled people used to lie—the blind, the lame, the paralyzed. One who was there had been an invalid for thirty-eight years. When Jesus saw him lying there and learned that he had been in this condition for a long time, he asked him, "Do you want to get well?"

"Sir," the invalid replied, "I have no one to help me into the pool when the water is stirred. While I am trying to get in, someone else goes down ahead of me."

Then Jesus said to him, "Get up! Pick up your mat and walk." At once the man was cured; he picked up his mat and walked.

The day on which this took place was a Sabbath....
—***John 5:1-9*** *(NIV)*

Jesus surveyed the people around the pool. No two looked the same. Some were lame. Some couldn't see. Each suffered from a different ailment, yet all of them were doing the same thing: waiting for the water to move. Once the waters stirred, the first in would be healed.

The Face of Hope

As the disabled waited, do you think that they were filled with hope? Or were they completely hopeless? What drove them to leave their homes or their spots begging on the street for pallets by the pool? There wasn't a single person there who didn't dream of being the first to the water and experiencing relief from his affliction, but only one person could touch the water first. They all hoped to be that one.

It is like buying a lottery ticket today. The odds against winning are ridiculous. Still, millions invest a bit of their grocery money for the chance to win. Why? It's hope.

The nature of hope defines what happens next in your life. Some people don't have money. Others feel that they don't have enough education. Perhaps they don't feel well or are exhausted. In this passage, a homeless and disabled man woke up in the morning filled with hope and acted on that optimism. That evening, he became a new person, healed and looking for work, because he did not let his condition suck the hope from his heart. He held on to the possibility that his life could be turned around.

Hope Today

Let's look at modern-day examples. Have you ever wondered how a woman who has endured a horrible divorce can pick herself up, dress in nice clothes, care for her mental and physical health, and focus on her emotional well-being? How does someone who has been damaged by a brutal separation act and look like she owns the world? How does she remain hopeful and not become bitter?

This is possible for someone who is filled with the hope found in the Lord's promise that He will heal and restore her and re-establish her purpose for His glory. Now, that may look like a newfound relationship, a second chance at marriage, or contentment in being right where she is. The point is that hope will be the catalyst.

On the other hand, those who lack hope often seem to be less careful about their appearances, not concerning themselves with proper hygiene, proper clothing, or weight. They grow bitter and find other damaged people who will validate their hopeless behavior.

Around the pool of Bethesda, the people knew that only one person in the entire crowd would be healed when the water was moved, yet they were hopeful and held on to the possibility of being that one person. That's why you don't quit going to church and other inspirational places. Life-changing messages may not hit you this week, but you can remain hopeful in God's goodness and trust that His life-changing Word will be revealed to you at the perfect time when you need it most.

That's why I'm in the pews every chance I get. I don't know when the message might move in my life, but I'm hopeful, so I'm going to look for it, never giving up. And I won't just sit in the pews and look for God's messages to me. If I had to, I would go across the world to look for them, wherever the Word of the Lord is spoken. But the hopeless aren't going to search for God. They'll stay at home, wishing.

Pretend that you and I are at the pool. I have a limp, and you can't move your arm. We're at the same location, but our conditions are different. Our life experiences have been different.

Your life is unique. Yes, you're going through a tough time. Perhaps it's divorce or gossipers or depression. Your experience doesn't have to define you. God has something special for you. If you hold on to that belief, it will give you hope.

How Long, Oh Lord?

We don't know how old the man at the pool was, but he'd been an invalid for thirty-eight years. For thirty-eight years, he waited, hopeful that one day he would be healed. For thirty-eight years, he cried out to Jehovah, "How long, oh Lord?"

This man came to the pool for thirty-eight years. That's hope. Did he have a church around him like you have, cheering him on? Probably not. People with disabilities were shunned. This brother was waiting for thirty-eight years, hopeful that he would be the one to reach the water first, and he waited alone.

How long have you been waiting? Whatever condition you have—and all of us have conditions—waiting is hard. I don't care how holy you are, you are waiting for something. What's your attitude while waiting?

This man was waiting when Jesus saw him lying there. Jesus knew that he had already been in that condition for a long time, and Jesus knows how long you've been wrestling with your problem. He knows whether you've been hoping for Him or ignoring Him.

When He comes to help, what's He going to see? Will He see you hoping for Him? He knows what you're going to do. He is holding you right now. Through whatever trial, His arms are around you. He embraced you before you were willing to be received. You need to understand that while you are waiting for a better job, a better house, a better group of friends, whatever, God knows that you've been waiting. That's why, when the time is right, He is going to show up just for you.

The man told Jesus the truth of his situation. He said, "Sir, I have no one to put me into the pool when the water is stirred. I have nobody. Someone beats me into the pool every time, but I've been hopeful for thirty-eight years."

The man was hopeful. He had to tell himself every day, "I know what I don't have. I know there is no help coming. But I'm not going to quit on my hope. I'm going to hope against all hope that one day I'll be healed. One day, someone will help me into the water."

But Jesus didn't help him into the water. He knew what the man wanted and what he needed. Jesus skipped a step. He did things differently from how the man thought He would. Jesus told the man, "Rise, take up your bed and walk" (John 5:8 NKJV). The man was healed instantly. He got up and walked (John 5:9).

While you're waiting, know that Jesus doesn't always fix things the way you think they should be fixed. He sometimes takes you straight to your destination.

I used to think that there was a negative in this story. I felt sorry for the man. But just as the man in this story did, I would wait thirty-eight years in my deformity to see Jesus' face and to have Him heal me.

As I wait, I'm not going to be frustrated. I know that He is coming. How do I know? First, He promised. Second, I have eyes to notice others being blessed. Some people get discouraged when they see others being blessed because they feel left out. But when I see these blessings, I know that God is in the blessing business and He is in my neighborhood. It gives me hope.

While you are waiting for your own deliverance to come, learn to celebrate the ones whose time it is to be blessed. Their blessings are not at your expense. You are not being rejected. Your time will come. Your waiting will be worth it. Learn to look around and celebrate who was chosen, who was number one, because you are number two. God's goodness toward others does not mean His injustice toward you.

Are You Owed Blessings?

Waiting and worrying sometimes come when you start believing that God owes you something, when you think that everything must come your way. I used to wonder how my kids could think that they should get special privileges just because they exist. Then I became a pastor, and I discovered that when people come to church, everybody becomes a kid, myself included. Most of us have some childish thoughts in our minds. We want to be number one, and we feel that we're owed blessings.

We know to raise our kids with the idea that they won't always get what they want when they want it, but when it comes to the things of God and the things of life, many of us become discouraged when it seems like God is blessing everyone except us. When we don't get what we want when we want it, we get frustrated with God. We become bitter and resentful, or we just give up.

But this man in the story said, "I know I don't have anyone to help me. I know I've been stuck here for thirty-eight years. But I'll tell you what has been happening. I am encouraged every time a brother steps in front of me and gets in the water before me and is healed. It makes me hopeful in a hopeless situation."

Even if it doesn't seem like God is doing something in your life at this moment, that doesn't mean you can't celebrate. God is moving in your neighborhood and helping those around you, just as He was helping others by the pool. Learn to celebrate the movement of God in the lives of others while you wait.

Don't be so down. You're not owed or promised anything other than that God will be there for you. Dress up and go out there and look like it's yours, like He is by your side. Your turn is coming, and soon you'll be the one who is blessed, the person God heals, and your testimony will be a blessing to others.

God watches you celebrating someone else. The message you're sending God when you celebrate others is that you don't think that you are better than anyone else. Have the same attitude that Jesus had. Although Jesus is equal with God, He humbled Himself, came down, and put on humanity (Philippians 2:5–8). God will always be attracted to humility.

I want to share three key points that will help you to wait without worrying.

1. If you are to wait without worrying, you must learn to give up your relationship with pain. Your pain is your closest companion, but you can choose to make your pain your excuse or your purpose. Risking your relationship with your pain means that you stop and think about how you perceive your pain.

The man at the pool who could not walk was thinking about something else, something other than his pain. He told Christ that there was no man to help him. He didn't sit and talk about his pain or complain about his crisis. And Christ simply said, "Get up." In other words, you must break up with your situation to embrace what Christ brings in. If you're not careful, you may become hopeless instead of being filled with anticipation while you are waiting.

Don't lose the purpose for the waiting. Always pray for the Spirit of God to empower you to lose your relationship with your situation. It is tough to leave what you know, but every waiting period will bring change in your life.

2. For you to wait without worrying, you must pray for the right attitude. It's not always about the best you can do. That's what the man by the pool said while waiting for his healing. He had the attitude that the best he could do was try to move himself, but someone always skipped over him.

Doing the best you can do may leave you dredged in the pain of waiting and worrying about failing. You think that it's your fault. You think that your best will never be good enough. If you are to wait without worrying, you need to understand that God must inject external help into your situation for you to be pumped up. He will get you ready so you can become the person you've been waiting to be.

It's not always about the best you can do because sometimes your best is not enough. When your best is not enough, the default behavior is worry. What should you do instead? You need to learn the right attitude by identifying the thoughts that help you. Not every thought is good for what you're waiting for. You're waiting for God, so think about Him and keep clinging to hope.

3. You must not deny your problem. Don't deny that your problem exists. If you do, you won't even go sit by the pool. Instead, deny your problem a place of influence over your life. If you deny that you have a problem, you're letting your problem dictate when God comes in, which will be never. I've got ninety-nine problems I know of, but denying my problems isn't one of them.

The man kept showing up to the pool as if to say, "I've been here, and I know nobody has been helping me. I've been rejected for thirty-eight years, but I will not deny my problem. And I will not allow my problem to have a place of influence in my life, or I will be held back by the anchor of a negative spirit." He acknowledged that he had a problem, and he kept showing up in hopes that God would take care of him. Learn from his example and keep showing up.

Positive Waiting

The Bible is full of people who waited. Abraham waited for God to bring him the covenant son (Genesis 18:1–19). Jacob grew tired of waiting for his inheritance, and he tricked Esau into selling his birthright (Genesis

25:19–34). David watched and waited for Bathsheba, and then he had her husband killed (2 Samuel 11). These are some of the examples in the Bible of those who messed up while waiting because they grew impatient. So, when you mess up during your waiting period, know that you are not the first one, but always pray that you will be ready for the help that will come from God.

God will help you to move over regular perceptions in your life. He will fix you so that you never miss when He shows up. Don't try to go it alone or fix things in your own way. If you stay focused on Him, you will notice the movement of God even when it's strange, even when it seems like He is saying ridiculous stuff.

When it's God moving, I don't mind waiting. The Bible says that "those who wait on the LORD shall renew their strength; they shall mount up with wings like eagles, they shall run and not be weary, they shall walk and not faint" (Isaiah 40:31 NKJV). David wrote, "Why, my soul, are you downcast? Why so disturbed within me? Put your hope in God, for I will yet praise him, my Savior and my God" (Psalm 43:5 NIV).

I will wait on the Lord. You, too, can wait without worrying.

WORKBOOK

Chapter One Questions

Question: Would you consider yourself a hopeful person or a hopeless person? What are some things, small or large, that you hope for? What are some areas where you have been waiting a long time and are tempted to give up hope?

_____
_____
_____
_____
_____
_____
_____
_____
_____
_____

Question: Jesus did things in a way the lame man did not anticipate. Rather than helping him into the pool, He healed him directly. Describe a time when God answered your prayers in a way that differed from your expectations. Read John 4:46–53 and John 9 for other examples of Jesus' help coming in a different way from what was expected or requested. What are you praying for right now, and are you open to God's answer in any form in which it may come?

_____
_____
_____
_____
_____
_____
_____
_____
_____
_____
_____
_____

Journal: How can you use the season of waiting you are in to grow closer to the Lord rather than to worry or whine? Write out some statements of truth about who God is and His faithfulness according to Scripture—for example, God is honest and does not lie (Numbers 23:19). When you are tempted to worry, meditate on these thoughts to help you stay focused on Him and keep the right attitude.

_____
_____
_____
_____
_____
_____
_____
_____
_____
_____

Action: Look around you to see the people whose prayers God is answering and in whose lives He is working. How will you celebrate with them, even as you wait in hope for your own answer? This could be as practical as giving a wedding gift or throwing a baby shower, taking someone to lunch to celebrate his or her new job or ministry, or helping a friend to move into a new home. How does it build your faith and hope to "rejoice with those who rejoice" (Romans 12:15 NIV)?

Chapter One Notes

CHAPTER TWO

Jesus Will Never Leave You

There is a God! He is lifted up on high and sitting in glory. He made the universe, the uncountable stars, and the galaxies. He created our world and made you in His image (Genesis 1:27). He made your five senses and a brain that can interpret information from your eyes, ears, nose, tongue, and touch, all at the same time.

He also came to earth in the form of His Son, Jesus, who lived the life of an average human being. He was humiliated, bullied, and so much more. He knows. He cried when His friend died (John 11:33–36). And He knows waiting. He waited thirty years before starting His ministry (Luke 3:23), thirty years for a three-year ministry with the greatest impact in all of history.

God knows everything, including your thoughts, and He knows what you are going through (Hebrews 4:13; Psalm 139). He has been there. Not only did He create everything, He also lived it. The good news is that He is by your side as you go through your trials (Hebrews 13:5–6).

When God brings a word, an assignment, or a person into your life, He knows what you need. He knows if you need to be there a little longer or if you have been in your situation long enough. God is not trying to catch you at your lowest to drag you down. He will equip you to be ready for the trials ahead and the waiting you must endure.

If you understand that God is in complete control and knows the future, you are going to discover that there is no lie the devil can use to discourage you. Jesus died on the cross because God knew that I would be a sinner. If I were not going to be a sinner, He wouldn't have needed to die. This makes your situation perfect. Why? Because He died for the sins you were going to commit. God says not to worry about what you've done (Psalm 103:12). Go forward and stop sinning. You're not too far gone for Jesus to work in your life.

Many people have the hardest time understanding that their past is covered by the cross. They are stuck perpetually waiting because they think that God can't use them. Have you ever noticed that in the Bible, God never asked people *why* they did it? You can walk with Him because He knows that you're a sinner and He took those sins and crucified them on the cross. They're gone, so walk with Him.

Why You Walk with Jesus

Jesus knows. Some preachers will tell you that He knows your mind, so keep it clean. He knows what you do in secret, so be careful. While this is true, it's not what the Bible chooses to talk about. Instead, it says that He is "closer than a brother" (Proverbs 18:24 NIV). He is by your side. What does that mean for you?

He knows your struggles and your pain. He knows that you don't like your job, that you are ill-treated at work, that you're not paid enough. Jesus knows if your friends are no good and getting you in trouble all the time. He knows if you're sick. He knows how unfair things are in society. Jesus knows that you need help because He sees you struggling, and He understands. That's how He sees us, but how do you see Him? It's how you see Him that determines how you behave around Him.

Remember the man who was crippled (John 5:1–9)? Jesus knew that he had been there for a long time. Jesus asked if he wanted to be made well. The sick man answered, and Jesus said, "Get up! Pick up your mat and walk" (John 5:8 NIV). The man told Jesus that he wanted to be made well. He didn't say, "Nah, skip me. Just go on to someone more deserving." This man knew his own condition and longed for relief.

Then the crippled man took a risk. Jesus commanded him to stand and walk. The man knew that if he wasn't healed, he would fall on his face when he stood up, yet he risked it and stood. That's faith. If you are to move in your waiting period, you must take risks by faith. As you wait and you walk with Him, you need to develop a healthy love for risk. Sometimes God is going to ask you to take risks. It takes faith, and if you're walking with Him, it's doable.

You must also get your attitude right. If you know that you need help, but there's nobody to help you, then why have you been here for thirty-eight years? The man by the pool showed his attitude by his actions. While he couldn't get in, he was still hopeful that his miracle would come. He knew that if he went home, it wasn't likely that he would be healed, so he stayed right there. He pitched his tent and lay on that ground for thirty-eight years. Why? Because he wasn't helpless; he was hopeful.

It doesn't matter what's pushing against you; you keep on believing. Why? Because you are a believer! Jesus is walking with you. It's not what you do; it's whose you are. When everybody has gone away, no matter what, you keep believing. When it doesn't make sense, you pitch your tent by the pool of Bethesda, and you keep on believing.

Recognize That He Is Beside You

I was driving to preach when the engine sputtered, then died. Thankfully, I made it to a gas station, but when I saw the setup, I paused. It was in "redneck country," and everybody was chewing tobacco and spitting everywhere. Ladies came around, all wearing pink dresses. I stood there with nothing to do. I looked down at the suit I was wearing in preparation for preaching. I was sure that I looked ridiculous to them. I didn't know where to hide.

The owner motioned for me to sit in his chair and told me to wait for whatever help was coming. As I sat there, watching people coming in to buy lotto tickets, I started talking to one guy about playing the lottery. I've never played, so I asked him, "What's the trick to playing lotto and coming close?"

He said something that blew my mind. He said, "Man, nobody plays lotto without believing they'll win. For some of us people who play lotto, we have more faith than you have in God."

I didn't understand, so I asked what he meant. He replied, "I tell them not to buy the ticket if you don't believe. You don't just throw in your dollar. You have hope and believe that winning is possible."

When you come to the Spirit of God, do you have the same faith? Do you believe? Do you go into the presence of God with the anticipation that perhaps today is your day? You have suffered and struggled, but maybe today is the day your family will come back or your job is going to flip over. Do you hold on to the belief that things will change? If you don't recognize that He is beside you, then you lose the belief. You lose the faith and the hope. When you are in a waiting place, be confident that Jesus is with you.

There are things you can do while you wait. Take up your worry and walk. Jesus is walking beside you. He has come to the pool and given you a command to move. So go. Act in alignment with your intentions and move. If you don't recognize that Jesus is with you, you will forget what the intention of the waiting is. You're at the pool of Bethesda, and you are not there to die. You went to the pool of Bethesda because your intention was to be healed. When God says to pick up your bed, remember your intention and why you've been in your position for so long.

God is not going to force you to do something you're not willing to do. He will never do anything in your life without your permission. That's why Jesus asked, "Do you want to be made well?" (John 5:6 NKJV). It's as if He were saying, "I can do it, but you've got the keys for Me to do it." He is not going to force the issue. Remember that He is walking with you, not grabbing you by the back of the neck and steering you. Jesus knows what you need. Remain focused on your purpose and intention so that you don't lose sight of God's power at work in your life.

Have you ever fought for something for so long that when you got it, you forgot why you were fighting for it? It's important to remember that He hasn't left you. Some people forget why they went to school, why the courses and classes were difficult, and why they graduated. By the time they graduated, they were caught up in the system. No matter what you go through as you work, don't ever forget the intent behind the waiting. That way, when the One with power and ability to transform your life shows up, you're ready to get up and obey what He says. If you recognize that He is walking alongside you, you won't lose sight of your goals.

How Do You Align Your Actions with Your Intentions?

As you wait, alignment is necessary so that worry will not control you. You align your actions with your intentions by selecting a replacement thought. Positive action often begins in the mind with a thought. When Christ told the man, "Rise, take up your bed and walk" (John 5:8 NKJV), this brother needed to select a replacement thought. Because of his circumstances, he would have been hardwired to think, "I can't walk." But instead, he chose to think, "This is the man who will help me. Perhaps this is the day I will walk."

Many people wait for things in life while their minds run rampant with thoughts of fear, disbelief, or failure. The problem occurs when you choose to be stuck in the same negative thought process without replacing your thoughts. If a person remains single for quite some time and then marries, the marriage may soon be in trouble if the single mindset remains. When you get married, you must select a thought that replaces the mindset of being single. This will help to promote a happy marriage.

You should select an empowering replacement thought because you will not always have the details to increase your faith. When God says that you are "the head and not the tail" (Deuteronomy 28:13 NKJV), it's going to require faith to live it.

Having faith means that even if you have no idea of the outcome, you will continue through the process anyway because you've seen the goodness of God in times before. When you have faith, you remind yourself and your thoughts of God's power to move on your behalf. You may not know what's going to happen, but this is your Father's world (Psalm 50:9–12). You may not know what He is going to do, but you must still move by faith in anticipation of blessings.

When the blessing arrives, accept it and bless Him. Why? Because it is your Father's world, so fill yourself up with faith. Yes, I've waited for some plans, but I never gave up. I had faith that the plan was going to come.

When you walk into a job interview, you must present

yourself with confidence and an attitude of belief that the job is for you. When you have the job and you want to rise, you hang out with managers and owners in order to learn their position so that you'll get promoted. It's intentional, every bit of it, and it's filled up with faith. It's amazing how Joseph, in every juncture of his walk, was always connected to someone in power where he was going (Genesis 37–50). He rose in prestige and power by connecting his actions with his intentions.

Don't shackle yourself with people who will avert your actions from your intentions. When you are surrounded by friends who don't have faith, it is the worst burden in your life. Instead, share your intentions with good friends, and the people around you will experience the joy of your hope turned into reality.

Check Your Faith Tank

Remember that you "walk by faith, not by sight" (2 Corinthians 5:7 ESV). Your faith tank should always be full. When we are waiting, many of us fill our tanks with worry instead of faith because of one of the following two issues.

1. When you are waiting, are you looking for enlightenment or entertainment? This makes a difference. Jesus enlightened the crippled man by saying, "Get up! Pick up your mat and walk" (John 5:8 NIV). In other words, "Get up, pack up, and keep walking." Revelation from God changed this man in an instant. After thirty-eight years lying down, there was still power in him.

The enlightenment came from a word from God. Every time you come to church, God has a word of enlightenment. But are you seeing church instead as a place of entertainment?

During the waiting period, God will always bring three things into your life: change, a choice, and a challenge. If you are waiting for anything, change will always be asked of you. If you are in the midst of change, you must choose what the change will look like. When the choice is made, the change will be a challenge.

Our culture is surrounded by visual stimulation and things that pull at our heartstrings, either through television, music, or cell phones. All of this entertainment can distract you from your purpose in God and drown out His voice in your life. Consider the choices you make in your life when you experience change. Will enlightenment or entertainment rule your thoughts when you are face to face with your challenge? Will you seek to be served or to serve?

2. Be filled up with faith because God is always intentional. Whatever God asks you to do, He is up to something. God has already figured this thing out. You may not know what God is up to, but He is intentional. Fill yourself up with faith because you need to understand that the days of waiting are temporary.

It doesn't matter what you've been through or how long you've been in it; all trouble is temporary. The only thing that counts is what you do *for* God, *with* God, and *through* God. Everything else is temporary. It may be long-lasting, but it's never everlasting. It's Jesus who is everlasting. Adversity can cause someone to break, but faith always breaks records. When you're filled with faith, the temporary is just that—temporary.

With faith, you learn to endure the process. Trust the process because you are secure in God's hands. God will never ask you to do anything if He has not already equipped you with the tools to succeed. That's where faith really shines, in trusting it all to Him.

God's Got This

Your feelings may be painful, but God has got this.

Your flesh may cry out, but God has got this. He is making you into a beautiful creation.

The righteous may fall seven times, but they will rise again. The wicked, however, will fall when disaster strikes (Proverbs 24:16). The righteous person is secure in the product God is making. Scripture says that "as far as the east is from the west, so far has he removed our transgressions from us" (Psalm 103:12 NIV). All you must do is confess your sin. God's got your sins covered. You can rise again.

Everybody is waiting on something. It may be a job, a change, a choice, or a challenge. The waiting period will always put you through trials. How are you waiting?

When Potiphar put Joseph in prison, Joseph didn't know how long that season would last. He was waiting, hoping to be set free. While he waited, the Lord was with him and granted him favor (Genesis 39:20–23). Even while Joseph was waiting in prison, he prospered.

The only thing that can shift your weakness to strength is the presence of Jesus Christ, and He will walk by your side if you let Him. Are you willing to make the choice for the change to become a reality? Whatever He is asking you to do is going to be a challenge to your flesh. God is not invested in your flesh; He is after your spirit. By working through the flesh, He is strengthening your spirit.

As He walks by your side, don't be afraid to ask Him for help. Cry out, "I'm anxious, Lord. Help me. Hear my cries. Keep me in Your everlasting right hand." Jesus says, "Be anxious for nothing…" (Philippians 4:6 NKJV), because He has got this.

We are marching to Zion, that beautiful heavenly City of God, but sometimes you must wait in unbearable places. God will trust you with this gift of waiting. Sometimes you will walk through valleys or deserts you don't want to cross. You'll face sickness you don't want to deal with. But keep in mind that He is always by your side. He will never leave you (Deuteronomy 31:6).

WORKBOOK

Chapter Two Questions

Question: Are you ready to walk forward with Jesus, or do you still feel bound by the mistakes from your past? How would you live differently if you believed and remembered that Jesus sees and knows all about your struggles, pain, grief, disappointments, failures, hopes, dreams, and fears?

_____
_____
_____
_____
_____
_____
_____
_____
_____

Question: Just as the crippled man picked up his mat and walked, what steps of faith can you take while you wait? What will prepare you to accept the answer God sends? What changes, choices, and challenges is this season of waiting requiring of you?

_____
_____
_____
_____
_____
_____
_____
_____
_____
_____

Journal: What are some prevalent doubts you have, and how can you replace each one with a faith statement that will propel you toward right thinking and positive action?

_____
_____
_____
_____

_____
_____
_____
_____
_____
_____
_____

Action: Write out and memorize Isaiah 40:30–31. As you quote it each day, fill in your own name to help you see how this promise applies to your life.

Chapter Two Notes

CHAPTER THREE

Servants in Training

There's a training process that takes place when you're young. You're told to sit down and wait for something or someone—for instance, for the teacher to prepare something, for the church service to end, or for the car to arrive at your destination. As you wait, you're not sure what will happen next. Then you're given a command that you're supposed to follow as quickly as the adult wants you to follow it, without wavering.

What do you do while you wait? Since you don't have your way and you're not sure what is next, you worry. You worry about how much play time you're missing out on; you fret over the lost hours of personal enjoyment.

You've been trained to worry while you wait, but you're missing an essential element now that you're older: God. He is the author of your waiting, and He does not want you to sit there quietly, waiting aimlessly. This is your training time. He is making you wait for a reason. Still, you're worried. Why?

He Hears Us

> *Now a certain man was ill, Lazarus of Bethany, the village of Mary and her sister Martha. It was Mary who anointed the Lord with ointment and wiped his feet with her hair, whose brother Lazarus was ill. So the sisters sent to him, saying, "Lord, he whom you love is ill." But when Jesus heard it he said, "This illness does not lead to death. It is for the glory of God, so that the Son of God may be glorified through it."*
>
> *Now Jesus loved Martha and her sister and Lazarus. So, when he heard that Lazarus was ill, he stayed two days longer in the place where he was.*
> —*John 11:1-6* (ESV)

Lazarus was sick, and his sisters knew what to do. They sent word to Jesus. Notice that they didn't tell Him what to do. Instead, they said, "Lord, the one you love is sick" (John 11:3 NIV). They knew that Jesus would know whom they were talking about and what He should do.

Likewise, you know what you want Him to do, but is demanding things from Him the best way to go about getting what you want? He is training you. You're not training Him. You're not going to tell Him what you want Him to do. Instead, you're going to tell Him what your problem is.

Why would you even try to tell Him what to do? Because you're worried that He won't do it your way. You're not trusting Him to build you the way He plans, a way that is better than anything you can imagine (Ephesians 3:20).

James 4:2–3 talks about your motives when you ask Him for things. Has He laid something on your heart, something specific? Have you talked to the Lord, knowing what you wanted to ask Him for, and ended up complaining to Him about what's wrong with your stuff? Have you told God about your problems and asked Him to help? James 4:2 says, "You do not have because you do not ask God" (NIV). If you are not specific in the asking, then things can go wrong. Whenever you come to God, you may create an atmosphere of frustration in your life because you are telling Him what's wrong and have no request of Him to make it better. You simply want to complain.

When the sisters reminded Jesus of His emotional connection to the one who was sick, Jesus listened. He heard them. I have good news for you: He hears you, too. There is a God big enough to deal with whatever you're going through, yet willing to come down to your level to hear you out. His ear is tuned to listening to you, and His purpose is to train you. Both are happening at the same time.

In this world, so many people are talking about problems with no solutions. There's either an effortless way out or no way out, but they keep repeating their issues to anyone who will listen. They're just dying to be heard. They don't need your money or your time; all they need is for you to hear them out.

Jesus heard the sisters and said that the sickness would not end in death (John 11:4). In other words, "You're calling Me because you are afraid of death, but I'm going to go beyond that. What happens next will be for the glory of God so that I, the Son of God, will be glorified through it." Do you see what He was doing? He was listening, yet the answer wasn't what they wanted. For Him to be glorified meant that they would have to wait.

When God waits, He is not waiting to embarrass or discourage you but because His glory moment has not fully arrived. He will show up and do what is best for everyone and get maximum glory.

He Wants You to Have Faith

What do you do when God says one thing and your story becomes another? God told the sisters to wait. They waited, and the one Jesus loved died (John 11:11–14).

When God says one thing and it becomes something other than what you're expecting, things can fall apart while you wait for God to hook you up with a divine revelation. When the one you love dies, you bury him and cry all you want, but you're still waiting.

The sisters buried their brother, sealed the tomb, and returned home (John 11:17). Even then, they were waiting. They had faith (John 11:21–27).

Perhaps you are in denial because of amnesia faith. You simply forgot what happened. It's buried and gone. Done. But real faith looks at situations and sees them for what they are. Lazarus was dead, and he needed to be buried.

In your life, there may be a Lazarus that needs to be buried, such as a job to quit or a relationship to move on from. It's time to step out in faith and move forward. Burying Lazarus didn't mean that their faith stopped. In fact, burying Lazarus proclaimed to the world that he was dead, truly gone, setting up the scene for what happened next.

Jesus went to the graveyard, asked them to open up the tomb, and called Lazarus out (John 11:38–43). He demanded that they unwrap him (John 11:44). People did what He said, even though they had no idea what would happen next. They moved in faith. Their faith was in training, and their faith was made whole when Lazarus came to life.

Even when you don't have all the facts, all the understanding of issues, all the points, and all the divine revelation of what God is up to, you've got work to do. How can you strengthen yourself during your time of training?

1. Rethink regular expectations. God is all-powerful. The only conflict is between you and your expectations of Him. God may sometimes choose to sacrifice your temporary convenience for His eternal purpose. The good news is that it's worth it in the end. Your faith will grow strong. But when you forget the bigger picture and set aside the higher purpose, your frustrations will come from wanting things your way. Then your worries take over. You tell God, "I need this," commanding God to restore your temporary convenience in a particular way.

Have you ever put your kids in the car and said, "We're going to Alabama!" The kids keep asking you, "Are we there yet? Huh? Are we? Are we there yet?" They have control issues. They can't drive. They don't know where they're going. They don't know when you're going to arrive or if you've already arrived. Waiting to get there causes them to be anxious or maybe even fearful of what they may encounter, so they whine and complain. Instead of just enjoying the journey, like counting how many red cars they see along the way, they whine about how long it's taking. This creates a conflict between the children and you, even though you know where you're going and how to get there and are focused on keeping everyone safe by driving carefully.

We do the same thing to God. He is in control, but instead of letting Him drive, we complain about the ride. We want to know when we'll get there. We ask for exits and detours. Instead, we should be enjoying the ride and training to go further so that He can take us on longer trips to more exotic locations.

2. God sacrifices your temporary convenience for His eternal purposes. God can deliver you from your trouble without taking you out of that trouble. You're safe. You're in His hands. You're already delivered although you are still in the same predicament. In other words, when God is up to His own divine purposes and plans for your life, what you are asking for is your relief, not in context but in consciousness.

Sometimes your relief is not in context because you want relief here and now. I've discovered that when you walk with the Lord and in the light of His Word, relief may not come in the way you imagined. Relief comes when His glory is upon us and we surrender to His purpose for our lives. Lazarus's sickness did not end in death even though he died. His death wasn't the end because Jesus brought him up from the dead. You shouldn't worry about your temporary inconvenience; it's not a loss. God is more than able to deliver you from a situation without actually taking you out of it.

The Bible says that Jesus delayed His trip to heal Lazarus for two days (John 11:6). We are not told that He was preaching or healing. We are not told that He was about His Father's business. We are just told that He waited.

When you love God and you are growing in your relationship with Him, you will learn that God does not share all the details with you. Many people will try to explain God, as if they understand why He is doing what He is doing. Have you ever had somebody try to explain God to you? If you can explain God, then He ceases to be God.

I've discovered in my walk with God that God is never on my time. His watch isn't like mine. Even so, God is always on time. He failed to come on my time, but you are here, reading this book, because He came in time.

3. Learn to stay in God's time zone. There are two time zones that you must deal with. You've got your time zone, and God has His own time zone. Suspend everything you have planned in your time zone and learn to stay in God's time zone, which means waiting on Him.

I've had the privilege of flying to various places in this world. When you move between time zones, your body is not built to switch quickly. You get jet lag, and it is torture. Worry then comes into play. Time zones are physical, just as much as waiting on God's timing is in the spiritual. It's best to learn to get into God's time zone.

God did what He had promised for thousands of years. Christ was born on time, in time, in the right place, in the right way. Christ came at the perfect time because God does all things perfectly in His time zone. It doesn't matter if your Lazarus is sick. Wherever life has you, God has you. In the meantime, just learn to connect with God's time zone.

Moses thought that he knew God's timing. He believed that he was to deliver God's people right away. An Egyptian was punishing an Israelite, and Moses felt that he had to do something right then, in his own timing. He killed the Egyptian (Exodus 2:11–12). Moses was not operating in God's time zone. Because of messing around in his own time zone instead of waiting on God's eternal purpose, Moses was kicked out of the country. He was a fugitive, declared an enemy of Egypt (Exodus 2:14–15). And it was quite some time before God used him for His purposes. There was far more training to do.

Ecclesiastes 3:1–8 puts it this way: "There is a time for everything, and a season for every activity under the heavens: a time to be born and a time to die, a time to plant and a time to uproot, … a time to tear down and a time to build, a time to weep and a time to laugh, … a time to scatter stones and a time to gather them, … a time to tear and a time to mend, a time to be silent and a time to speak…" (NIV). Most of us are waiting for a time to harvest, forgetting the rest, and we worry while we wait.

Worry becomes the default emotion when you are in the wrong time zone. Not everything can be done immediately. What time is it? That's not the question you have to ask yourself. What matters is *whose* time it is, yours or His.

You can learn to wait on the Lord. He is training you,

and that takes faith. When your faith in Him is strong, you're able to hold on for His timing without worrying because you know whose hands hold your future. God's mighty finger traces a path through time, and as a servant in training, you simply need to wait. Wait on the Lord. I'll say it again: Wait!

WORKBOOK

Chapter Three Questions

Question: Read Isaiah 55:8–9. Do you tell God how to answer your prayers, or do you tell Him about your needs and wait for *His* answer? Do you want God to fulfill your plans more than you want to fulfill His? Think about the three things you pray about most often. How can you change the way you pray to be more concerned about God's glory than your agenda?

_____

_____

_____

_____

_____

_____

_____

_____

Question: How have you been training during your season of waiting? In what ways are you growing and learning? How is your walk with God becoming stronger? How can you move yourself from your time zone to God's?

_____
_____
_____
_____
_____
_____
_____
_____
_____
_____

Journal: Who or what is a "Lazarus" that has died in your life? Have you acknowledged the loss and buried it? How did this loss conflict with your expectations of who God is or how He would act? Have others tried to explain God to you? What are you learning about how God works and who He really is?

_____
_____
_____

_____

_____

_____

_____

_____

_____

_____

_____

_____

_____

Action: In a small group setting, have each person who is willing describe a time when God didn't do things in his or her timing. How did each person experience God's perfect timing? How can sharing these experiences help you to wait in faith instead of worrying? Read about Joseph, Moses, David, and Esther in the Old Testament. What do the lives of these people of faith teach you about God's timing and waiting without worrying?

Chapter Three Notes

CHAPTER FOUR

Knowing God's Divinity

The power of Jesus coming to find that Lazarus had died must be seen in its context for you to understand completely how waiting and worrying affect you.

> *On his arrival, Jesus found that Lazarus had already been in the tomb for four days. Now Bethany was less than two miles from Jerusalem, and many Jews had come to Martha and Mary to comfort them in the loss of their brother. When Martha heard that Jesus was coming, she went out to meet him, but Mary stayed at home.*
>
> *"Lord," Martha said to Jesus, "if you had been here, my brother would not have died. But I know that even now God will give you whatever you ask."*
>
> *Jesus said to her, "Your brother will rise again."*
>
> *Martha answered, "I know he will rise again in the resurrection at the last day."*
>
> *Jesus said to her, "I am the resurrection and the life. The one who believes in me will live, even though they die; and whoever lives by believing in me will never die. Do you believe this?"*

"Yes, Lord," she replied, "I believe that you are the Messiah, the Son of God, who is to come into the world."

After she had said this, she went back and called her sister Mary aside. "The Teacher is here," she said, "and is asking for you." When Mary heard this, she got up quickly and went to him. Now Jesus had not yet entered the village, but was still at the place where Martha had met him. When the Jews who had been with Mary in the house, comforting her, noticed how quickly she got up and went out, they followed her, supposing she was going to the tomb to mourn there.

When Mary reached the place where Jesus was and saw him, she fell at his feet and said, "Lord, if you had been here, my brother would not have died."

When Jesus saw her weeping, and the Jews who had come along with her also weeping, he was deeply moved in spirit and troubled. "Where have you laid him?" he asked.

"Come and see, Lord," they replied.

Jesus wept.

Then the Jews said, "See how he loved him!"

But some of them said, "Could not he who opened the eyes of the blind man have kept this man from dying?"
—John 11:17–37 (NIV)

We all experience the loss of a loved one at some point in our lives. Jesus, Mary, and Martha lost Lazarus. If you keep living in this world, you're going to lose someone or something you love. The Lazarus in your life may be a person, a job, a situation, or something else.

When God allows your Lazarus—something you love—to die, the harsh reality, from a human perspective, is that you bury your dead so life can move forward. Learn to begin it, learn to end it, and do whatever you must within the funeral period. For some of us, it may be dreams that die. For God to resurrect anything, it must die and be buried. It can't be resurrected if it didn't die and wasn't buried. The miracle that you are waiting on God to do in your life requires things to be sealed in tombs.

Understanding God

If God tells you everything that is going to happen, then you don't need faith. Hebrews 11:6 says that "without faith it is impossible to please God" (NIV). Without faith, you won't grow in Him. Mary's and Martha's patience and faith were tested.

Jesus' title of *Immanuel* means "God with us" (Matthew 1:23). Some call Him healer, deliverer, provider, righteous, a friend, "the bread of life" (John 6:35 NIV), or "living water" (John 4:10 NIV). These names describe our Lord and His power to work in our lives. What's in your name? What is your job description? Like mine, I'm sure that it falls short of His.

I've learned that when the Lord delays His coming in my situation, it's not an excuse to take matters into my own hands. When my life is not going as I want, I should not attempt to manipulate the situation. His name is *Immanuel*. Even when I'm not getting what I want, He is with me. His job description covers me. Don't try to take matters into your own hands.

Look closely at how Jesus spoke with Martha. She snapped off a quick comment that if Jesus had been there, Lazarus would have lived. Was she blaming Him? Martha said something dumb, and Jesus had to explain why. Before you get too hard on Martha, keep in mind that we've all said unfaithful and silly things. It dawned on me how many dumb things I've done and said myself. There are moments when I thought that I knew better than God what He should have done.

Jesus' grace and mercy allow Him to ignore your

assumptions so that He can minister to you. God looks past your pride so that He can deal with your real need. God will meet you where He finds you. That's who God is. Instead of you trying to reach Him, He will find you where you are. Life will take you places and sometimes leave you lost, hopeless, and unable to find your own way. But God isn't going to leave you. He is going to find you.

Life will take you, like the prophet Elijah, to a cave, hungry and tired (1 Kings 19:9). If you were to ask Jonah, he would tell you that life can take you to the belly of a stinking fish (Jonah 1:17). God found them. *Immanuel* means "God with us." He will never abandon you, so continue to seek Him and remain steadfast in your faith.

Paul said in Romans 3 that no one is righteous without God. Humanity is running our own way, running to destruction, yet God came to us. Mary and Martha didn't go where Jesus was. They asked Him to come to them. No matter how life shakes you down or how successful you are, it is not you who makes it to God. He will meet you wherever He finds you.

Receive His Divinity

"If you had been here, my brother would not have died" (John 11:21 NIV). Those words from Martha must have turned the balmy air in Israel cold. Her bitter words were thrown to the earth before God. Part of her attack addressed the humanity of Jesus, and another addressed the divinity of Jesus. His understanding was perfect. Christ told her, "I am the resurrection and the life. ... Do you believe this?" (John 11:25–26 NIV). In other words, could she rise above His humanity and see His divinity? Mary worshipped Him, but could Martha?

Bitterness and frustration at God can creep in during seasons of waiting. The temptation to feel anger is real. As you wait on God to move in your situation, learn to see past the humanity of Jesus and receive His divinity. I know that you cling to the idea that He walks with you and talks with you; this is His humanity. But His divinity told the lame to walk, commanded the blind to see, and forgave the woman at the well.

While Jesus' humanity reaches you, His divinity rescues you. His humanity comes down to where you are, but His divinity lifts you up to where He is. His humanity comes to touch you, and His divinity comes to transform you. He is human to comfort you and divine to change you. He is human to cry with you, and He is divine to wipe away every tear. Learn to see beyond His humanity and receive His divinity.

Worship in the Waiting

Christ is with you even when you are distracted. He is with you when you feel discouraged, both in life and in your walk with God. In Exodus, we read that the children of God lost their way on their journey to the promised land. As you walk on your own journey, there will be momentary distractions that pull you away from Him. When this happens, notice that God doesn't embarrass you or harass you. Instead, He carefully draws you to worship Him.

Don't lose your worship. It's easy to worship when times are light and your burdens are easy. Mary was a worshipper when there were no problems, and it carried over into the times when it was hard to worship. If you don't worship when times are easy, then worshipping when times are hard is nearly impossible. What you do before trouble comes is what sustains you when trouble arrives. In Daniel 6, Daniel was delivered by the prayers and worship he offered before he was in trouble, and when he was in trouble, he offered praise and worship.

God was good when Lazarus was well. He was also

good when Lazarus was sick. He was good when Lazarus died, when there was a funeral, when he was laid in a tomb. He was still good when Lazarus's body was decaying four days later. He was good when He wept. He was good before He called Lazarus out and after. God is good when everything is good *and* when things are bad.

Keep your worship and anchor your faith in a relationship with His divinity rather than His humanity. Knowing God's divinity is a powerful tool when you are waiting. Lean on His divinity, not just His humanity. Learn more about His character and let go of bitterness. Then the time of waiting will train you to be powerful as you walk with Him without worrying.

WORKBOOK

Chapter Four Questions

Question: Describe a time when you felt angry at God, talked back to Him, or thought that He had failed you. How have you experienced God showing you mercy and finding you when you were too crushed by life to seek Him?

_____

_____

_____

_____

_____

_____

_____

_____

_____

_____

Question: What does your life look like when you try to take control rather than allowing God to be in control? Give some examples of people from the Bible who faced ongoing consequences for refusing to wait on God's plan and jumping in to try to fix the situation themselves.

_____
_____
_____
_____
_____
_____
_____
_____
_____
_____

Journal: In what ways do you need to connect with Christ's humanity, and in what ways do you need to believe in His divinity? How does each speak to your current needs, hurts, and hopes?

_____
_____
_____
_____

_____

_____

_____

_____

_____

_____

_____

Action: Set aside a few hours to spend alone with God in a time of worship. You may want to have with you a prayer journal, a worship playlist, selected scriptures, or lists of His attributes and names. Use these tools to prepare your heart to praise Him. Be still in His presence and seek Him rather than His solutions for your problems.

Chapter Four Notes

CHAPTER FIVE

When Blessings Delay

Blessings come in so many packages that you simply can't count them all. For one family in 1 Samuel 1, the blessing was a child who would shake the foundations of Israel. While this child would change the world, it took some time for him to come. *They had to wait.* Their lessons teach us how to wait when blessings take time to come.

Elkanah was from Ramathaim Zophim in Ephraim. He had two wives. Now, you must understand that sometimes in the Old Testament, you see people doing things that don't jive with your perception of right and wrong. As a culture, we are a learning and growing people of God. Every biblical description is not a biblical prescription. They had two or more wives back then, and that was between them and God. It's not your role to judge.

One wife, Peninnah, had children. Hannah, the other wife, had no children. What made the situation more interesting was that Elkanah, the husband, favored the childless Hannah over Peninnah. Can you guess that the two wives didn't like each other much? Peninnah had a positive outcome in life, and Hannah had a negative outcome. Their story goes together. Hannah, the childless negative, saw Peninnah as the positive.

That's how life goes. There will always be a negative and a positive. That means there's a place to go, a way to get better and move forward from negative to positive. However, you can't move forward without Christ. He is the one who moves you from negative to positive. God never lets a wall get in your way without a door, but there is always a wall. In this case, Hannah's negative was that she was childless, and Peninnah was provoking Hannah ruthlessly.

Elkanah seems to have let Peninnah hurt Hannah, even though Hannah was his favorite of the two. But he did sacrifice to the Lord, and he took them to worship in Shiloh. Year by year, when they went up to the house of the Lord, Peninnah continued to tear at Hannah. Hannah wept bitterly and did not eat. So cruel was Peninnah that not even the holy house of the Lord, that sacred space, could stop her from hurting Hannah (1 Samuel 1:6–7). As you can see, not everybody coming to worship comes for the right reason. Peninnah used the opportunity to be cruel to Hannah. That was the height of profaning God and sacred worship.

Was Hannah's barren womb her fault? Was there a sin in her past that caused her to be infertile? Of course not. True, there were sins in her past—there are sins in everyone's past—but every challenge in your life is not a consequence of an unwise decision. Scripture says that God had closed Hannah's womb (1 Samuel 1:5). God did not lay a time of testing on her because she had sinned, but because her faith was to be strengthened.

Is It Your Fault?

You might have been told by life and by people that you must have done something wrong to deserve your fate and you are being punished. If you're tempted to believe that, look at Job, who "was blameless and upright" before God (Job 1:1 NIV). He lived right, talked right, and worshipped right, and it wasn't his fault that his life fell apart. God was using him to prove a point to Satan. That's why you cannot trust everybody's opinion on your life. When they see you limping, they think that you've failed. They don't understand that your limp came from the time He touched you (Genesis 32:22–32).

Because your time of trials is so hard, it's tempting to convince yourself that it will last forever. Remember that you're in training. The days of trouble are always temporary. You might be in Egypt for 430 years, but it's temporary. It doesn't matter how long it is; it's not forever. These are my five favorite words in Scripture: "And it came to pass..." (Exodus 12:41 NKJV). It means that nothing comes to stay. Everything passes. Good or bad, nothing lasts forever. Even the worst days can't last forever.

Don't make temporary situations permanent. God gave Israel peace when they repented (Judges 3:11). They thought that the peace would last forever. Forty years of peace may feel like forever when you're living it, but it doesn't last forever. It's temporary. The tough times are temporary as well. I wish I could have told Hannah that her situation was a passing season.

Sometimes when you're down, everything looks bad. Hannah was devastated, yet she was well taken care of, had a husband who loved her, and had a perfect God. In the valleys of waiting, depression can make everything look awful. Does it feel like your life has been just plain bad? Do you have parents? A spouse? A friend? Is your belly full? Is your thirst quenched? Are you under a shelter? Not everything is bad. If you think things over, you will discover that there are some roses for you to smell. There is hope. There are good things in your life, and the bad things are temporary.

Watch carefully that you don't walk around as if God owes you a debt. Do you think that Hannah felt like God owed her a child? If you believe that God owes you, your attitude toward God will make you a miserable person to be around. You'll stink like the entitled person you are. Why keep feeling this way? You know that God has been good to you. Don't allow your longing for more to keep you from being grateful for what you already have from God.

Don't Be Discouraged by the Process

People tell me, "You have no idea what I'm going through." That may be true, or I could have an idea because I've been through a lot. One thing I'm sure of: we all can be discouraged by the process, the grind, the waiting, the training.

The truth of the matter is that your healing is in the hands of God. In Psalm 121, the psalmist looks to the mountains and asks where his help comes from. Does it come from the rocks, hills, or mountains? No, help comes from the Lord. So, why give up before the Lord shows His mighty hand in your life? Don't miss it by letting discouragement draw you away from the goal.

Timing is everything in the economy of waiting. Moses felt as if he had to kill that Egyptian because of the calling on his life (Exodus 2:11–15). David didn't understand that God had to prepare him in a season of waiting in hiding so he could develop the patience that would be needed to lead a stiff-necked people (1 Samuel 19–31).

Joseph's brothers threw him into a pit (Genesis 37:23–24). He might have thought that pit was the last place he'd ever see, but God got him out. He was sold into slavery, but he was promoted repeatedly (Genesis 37:25–28, 36; Genesis 39:1–6). He was sitting comfortably in the big house, but that door was closed, and he was thrown in prison (Genesis 39:6–20). Was the prison the last door? No, there was more to the process. God took him to Pharaoh's house, placed him in the palace, where he wore the wardrobe of the most powerful man in the world (Genesis 41).

Waiting when a door is closed and hoping that another is being opened is what you do. You don't know God's timing and provision. God is more concerned with your character development than His display of power. He is willing to wait until you've developed into a person who can lead people, a person who can stand with a pharaoh.

Do you know how good God is? He kept your heart ticking while you were asleep, snoring. How many times do you blink your eyes without your consent? God lets trees rest in the winter, looking dead, and when spring arrives, He fills them with life. In seasons when all hope seems lost, God is developing your character. If you get the blessing before your character is ready, the blessing might kill you.

I tell my kids that everything I have is theirs: my money, my house, my car. But if I were to give them the keys to drive the car now, I would be killing them. They're too young. They would crash and be killed. I am a loving father, and I don't want to see them hurt. When they are ready for the blessing, I will train them. When their character fits the blessing, then they can drive.

Hannah wasn't ready for the blessing of a child. She had to wait. Knowing that God has a perfect view of your character and the future will add comfort to your waiting. Knowing that the challenge won't last forever will help you through the time of waiting.

Elkanah was worried about Hannah (1 Samuel 1:8). She was his favorite of his two wives, and his wife who had his children was picking on her. He asked her why she was crying. Why wasn't she eating? Why was her heart broken? He had worked hard to make her happy, trying to be worth ten sons, yet she still wept.

Elkanah didn't deny that Hannah was crying and not eating. He brought in another perspective: "There is something better, and it's me." As prideful as this may sound, it worked because he was doing all he could to be worthy. She ate and felt a little better. She took care of her physical needs and was ready to keep worshipping.

Hannah went into the temple to pray, and the priest, Eli, watched her pray. He saw her tears and watched her lips moving, but he couldn't hear her. She made a vow that if God remembered her and gave her a son, no razor would touch his head to cut his hair (1 Samuel 1:9–12).

Eli watched her lips. Hannah was speaking in her heart, so her lips moved without words coming out. Eli thought that she was drunk. He told her to put away the wine and was disgusted by her (1 Samuel 1:13–14).

Worship in the Time of Need

Real worship has always been misunderstood. People want to know how they can tell if God has heard their prayer. When it's fervent, you know.

There are biblical examples of people who called upon God and were misunderstood because of their focus on Him. David danced before the Lord (2 Samuel 6:14–15). He worshipped with such abandon that his wife, who was looking through the window, was mad at him and told him that he was an embarrassment (2 Samuel 6:16, 20). Because she misunderstood David's worship, God locked her womb (2 Samuel 6:23).

How frustrated must Hannah have been? She prayed to God, and the priest thought that she was drunk. He had the guts to come over and give her counseling at once. He didn't even wait for her to say amen before he told her to stop drinking. He simply thought that he was going to fix her.

If you want your worship to be understood, you're going to miss your shout. Some issues in your life must be understood only by the one you are talking to, and that's God. There may be people around you who don't get it. Don't allow their doubts to distract you or detract from your focus on God. Hannah didn't come to give a promise to the priest; she came to make a vow to the Lord.

Notice that Hannah had a deep need. She came to talk to God, to fall before Him and plead. You can get messed up when you come to the house of God and you think that you have no need for God. You could be there just to be entertained and have an enjoyable time. You could pretend that you're there to worship, but really you just want to be seen.

Hannah answered Eli. She said, "No, my lord, I am a woman of sorrowful spirit. I have drunk neither wine nor intoxicating drink, but have poured out my soul before the LORD" (1 Samuel 1:15 NKJV). Eli got it. He understood. She was honest about her predicament, and he replied, "Go in peace, and the God of Israel grant your petition which you have asked of Him" (1 Samuel 1:17 NKJV). Relieved, Hannah started caring for herself again (1 Samuel 1:18).

When you wait on God, you wait with expectancy. Your prayers should reflect your faith in God's purpose and provision for your life. When you talk to God, do it with confidence. God loves you and wants to bless you, so what happens when the blessings do pour in?

WORKBOOK

Chapter Five Questions

Question: What are some difficulties in your life that you have faced through no fault of your own? Have others tried to tell you that you are to blame for those challenges? Do you believe that your situation is permanent or temporary, and how is that belief evidenced in how you live?

_____
_____
_____
_____
_____
_____
_____
_____
_____

Question: Like Elkanah, are you watching a loved one suffer through the pain of disappointment, uncertainty, or grief? What are some ways you can offer your presence, support, and hope to this person as he or she waits on the Lord?

_____
_____
_____
_____
_____
_____
_____
_____
_____
_____
_____
_____

Journal: God is more concerned with your character development than His display of power. Write out ways your character is being developed through this season of waiting. What are some areas where you need to submit to the work God wants to do *in* you, even as you wait for what He will do *for* you?

_____
_____
_____

_____

_____

_____

_____

_____

_____

_____

_____

Action: Make a list of blessings you are thankful for and take time to tell God (and others) how much you appreciate these good things in your life. Review your list when you are tempted to think that everything is all wrong or that your life is all difficulties.

Chapter Five Notes

CHAPTER SIX

A Willing Participant

Hannah continued to worship, and God answered her prayer. Hannah's face was no longer sad because she was pregnant with a son (1 Samuel 1:20). God now trusted her faith. He had tested her soul, and she was ready. Her time of waiting was over, her training was complete, and she was capable of being a mother who would have to make an important sacrifice.

Trust

People need to feel that they are trusted, but how can a person be trusted if he or she hasn't been tested? How do you show that you understand the material in school if there's no exam? It begins with a small step. When the faithful servant multiplied his master's wealth, the master said, "Well done, good and faithful servant! You have been faithful with a few things; I will put you in charge of many things" (Matthew 25:14–30 NIV).

This can be true for more than just God. You can take God's lead on this. To all the singles reading, you cannot trust a man or a woman whom you haven't tested. It's the same thing with pastors and members. If you have a little conflict, how far do they go, how far do they fall away from the church?

God is saying that your trouble isn't going to kill you. Your trouble is to qualify you so that you can be trusted. When the trust comes, the blessings will follow.

Trust goes both ways. If God is going to trust you, both He and you must know that you can be trusted. How do you know that you can be trusted if you haven't proven it to yourself? You must trust Him. God knows.

Perhaps you're praying incorrectly. Perhaps you're praying that God will take away the conflict. Where God is, there is no defeat. Where God is, there are no mistakes. Where God is, everything works out. Your trouble is a matter of trust. You can't be the manager and not want to deal with a crisis that comes to qualify you. Nobody makes a manager of someone who cannot handle conflict. For you to become a manager, your boss must see how you handle people when you're under pressure. If you are praying for your conflict to get out of your way, you are sweeping away any chance of promotion. You need to be tested against contentious people.

Look at the promotion and training of Joseph in the Bible. He could handle all the slaves, the food distribution, the government, and all the other things that came with running an empire (Genesis 41). But first, he was tested to lead his peers (Genesis 40). Potiphar's wife came in and shattered Joseph's quick rise (Genesis 39:6–20), but he rose even further by allowing the time of testing instead of praying it away. Don't worry about how God will get you out of a situation; just keep praying.

What are you accomplishing while rising above what was designed to crush you? That's where the true glory grows and is directed to God. You tell your children, "You can be anything." I want to tell you that you can be anything your character allows you to be.

Nothing Is Bigger Than Your Awareness of God

Being aware of God's presence in your life doesn't happen naturally. Finding Him in everything is a trained behavior.

I've always wondered why God doesn't always speak when we need Him to say something. If God were to say, "I've got you!" that would be enough. But sometimes God is silent, especially when He is leading you to places of deeper trust.

It seems as if my life is designed to attract trouble of one kind or another, but I don't pray trouble away. I believe that the evidence of God's presence always outweighs the proof of His absence. Even if you are in a situation where God hasn't said anything to you, it doesn't mean that He is not speaking. Learn to fall in love with His presence because God will always show you, affirm to you, that He is there.

When Hannah did not have a child, she went to the temple, seeking the presence of God. Even though the priest didn't understand her and thought she was drunk, the fact that the priest engaged her was evidence of the presence of God. Without God, why would the priest have bothered?

I find it impossible to believe that God is *not* with me, even if I haven't heard from Him, because I've learned to sense His presence, acknowledge Him, and see His handiwork in everything. I've learned to believe Him without the sound of a booming voice or an angel standing in front of me because His presence is always there.

You can see His presence when you refuse to be impressed by the size of your problem. Don't make your problem bigger than your belief. Acknowledge your problem and its size, but don't be impressed by it. What happened with David when Goliath made his challenge (1

Samuel 17)? What if David had run away because Goliath was a big man? Instead, when little David came in, he said, "Who is this uncircumcised Philistine that he should defy the armies of the living God?" (1 Samuel 17:26 NIV). Goliath was a giant, but David refused to be impressed by his size. Goliath came with power and size and strength, but David knew his God. David might not have known how God was going to do it, but he had faith that God would make a way.

Your faith is impacted when you become addicted to the size of your problems. People ask, "How are you doing?" "Fine" is a satisfactory answer. It's pregnant with meaning, but is it enough? Nobody has time for all the details of how you're doing. You're not faking it; you've just learned that you're not going to allow the size of your trouble to impress you. You've learned to function above your dysfunction because if somebody needs help, you've got something to give. You're not going to let your struggles stop you from helping.

Trouble is not a competition, so don't trade talk on your troubles. Trouble comes in proportion to the purpose and gift God has given each of us. In order for you to be anchored and centered, God must give you enough trouble to balance your emotional scale. If He doesn't give you trouble, then your head gets bigger. If He gives you more than you can handle, then you will call on Him. He must give you problems in proportion to your gifts.

Hannah was barren because there was a gift coming to the nation, and that gift was Samuel. Hannah had to be the kind of mother a child this powerful needed. Because of her trials, she was, and her child grew to change the world. Do you see how the greater the gift is, the greater the trial is? Hannah wasn't impressed by the size of the problem. She focused on the bigger picture.

When I was a little boy, whoever was sick in the family was treated better than everybody else. If you were sick, that was the only time you could sleep in your parents' bedroom. When you were sick, Momma would put her hand on your forehead and would pray. She would do the chores if it was your duty to clean the place.

In fact, if you were sick, Momma would ask, "What do you want to eat?" You might just want ice cream. Ice cream might have nothing to do with your sickness, but because you were sick, Momma was going to get you ice cream. Momma wanted to watch over you. She would mend you.

Learn to take God at His word. When He says that He will care for you and bring you ice cream, believe it. If God says that it is so, you don't need evidence or proof first. It'll happen. And if you get addicted to the Word of God and neglect the world, you will be able to do some amazing things.

After a trial, it's easy to forget God and go back to the world. Why do young people do that more than older folks? Because trials come and go, and the older you are, the more you know that you need to stay connected to God. You're going to need Him again.

God must give you mountains to keep you encouraged, and He must give you valleys to keep you humble. Both the mountains and the valleys are places where you learn. It must happen: mountain, valley, mountain, valley. You can't prolong one phase of your life because you like it. It's temporary.

When I talk to young people looking all fine, gorgeous, and wonderful, I say, "You need to look at these senior ladies in the house. They used to look like you. You must enjoy the season. Roll with it." Older folks don't need the looks because they've got the experience and the brains. My daughter often tells me, "Daddy, I can't wait to be a teenager." I tell her, "You need to understand that there are issues with being a teenager. You'll get there. Keep on eating and sleeping and playing. You will get there before you know it."

Finish What You Begin

The journey starts with a promise that God will be with you. Then the trials start, the training and the waiting. And then you end up right back where you started. What's changed? You've been blessed and trained, and now you're closer to God because of it.

When God gives you a promise instead of an answer, it reveals His desire to draw you into your eternal purpose. Eli told Hannah, "Go in peace, and may the God of Israel grant you what you have asked of him" (1 Samuel 1:17 NIV). When you embrace the process of the promise over the answer, it gives you the privilege of being part of the answer.

Because Hannah embraced the process, she had the privilege of becoming part of the answer. The Bible says that Hannah's family rose early in the morning, worshipped before the Lord, and returned to their home (1 Samuel 1:19). Hannah stood on the promise that she was going to have a baby. She went home and trusted God, and she took the steps necessary to make the promise happen.

Every blessing of God will enlist your participation. You must go all in. That's part of waiting and finishing. Many people don't understand that in order to receive your blessing, you must participate in the process of its manifestation. Without participation, you are putting off the blessing. You cannot forgive somebody or reconcile with somebody if you don't talk to that person. You must be willing to participate in the process before God will heal you and move you forward.

What are you willing to do for the promise? Maybe you want to restore a relationship with your estranged parents so that you no longer feel abandoned or alone. Maybe you want to experience joy in your life instead of spending your days and nights feeling depressed and hopeless. Are you willing to participate in the process to the fullest?

In his famous devotional *My Utmost for His Highest*, Oswald Chambers stated, "If, however, we do something simply to overcome our depression, we will only deepen it. But when the Spirit of God leads us instinctively to do something, the moment we do it the depression is gone. As soon as we arise and obey, we enter a higher plane of life."[1]

Here's the main question that comes across my desk most times and holds people back: "Why me?" The answer is "Who else but you?" With everything that you are experiencing right now, you are participating in the results you are getting—the good, the bad, the ugly, you name it.

So, why you? You've already been enlisted. Embrace the journey. Enjoy the ride. Be the person God intends you to be and learn to trust His timing.

WORKBOOK

Chapter Six Questions

Question: What are some tests that you expect people in different professions—such as athletes, politicians, teachers, and business leaders—to go through before they are proven and trusted? What happens if someone who has never faced conflict or challenge is placed in a position of prominence? How is the testing in your life for your own benefit?

_____

_____

_____

_____

_____

_____

_____

_____

_____

Question: What are some practical ways you can keep an awareness of God's presence in your life every day? How can you replace obsession over the size of your problem with worship over the size of your God?

_____

_____

_____

_____

_____

_____

_____

_____

_____

_____

Journal: Chart some of the mountains and valleys in your journey with God. How have the mountains encouraged you? How have the valleys humbled you? What have you learned through each of them?

_____

_____

_____

_____

_____

_____

_____

_____

_____

_____

_____

Action: What are some practical things you can do now to participate in your blessing? In what areas have you been procrastinating when you need to act? What have you stopped doing that you need to resume? What have you started doing that you need to stop?

Chapter Six Notes

CHAPTER SEVEN

Waiting in the Unbearable

Sometimes it's easy to see the blessings of other people—that is, until we're the ones being blessed. Then we realize how much this blessing will change our lives and how much responsibility there will be. For example, imagine explaining to your fiancé that while you're still a virgin, you're going to have a baby, and that baby is God. That's what happened to Mary.

> *In the sixth month of Elizabeth's pregnancy, God sent the angel Gabriel to Nazareth, a town in Galilee, to a virgin pledged to be married to a man named Joseph, a descendant of David. The virgin's name was Mary. The angel went to her and said, "Greetings, you who are highly favored! The Lord is with you."*
>
> *Mary was greatly troubled at his words and wondered what kind of greeting this might be. But the angel said to her, "Do not be afraid, Mary; you have found favor with God. You will conceive and give birth to a son, and you are to call him Jesus. He will be great and will be called the Son of the Most High. The Lord God will give him the throne of his father David, and he will reign over Jacob's descendants forever; his kingdom will never end."*

> *"How will this be," Mary asked the angel, "since I am a virgin?"*
> —**Luke 1:26–34** *(NIV)*

This was not an ordinary blessing that a pastor, a rabbi, or a priest brings with him. This was a blessing that an angel, who was dispatched from glory, brought with him. This was not just any angel, but one whose name is well known. Gabriel is one of the few angels in Scripture announced by name.

Gabriel came in and greeted Mary with power: "Rejoice, highly favored one, the Lord is with you; blessed are you among women!" (Luke 1:28 NKJV). Before He even arrived, Mary knew that Jesus was not going to be a normal child. Gabriel told her, "He will be great, and will be called the Son of the Highest; and the Lord God will give Him the throne of His father David. And He will reign over the house of Jacob forever, and of His kingdom there will be no end" (Luke 1:32–33 NKJV).

Mary heard this promise, and she just had to know how it would come about. Isn't it funny that when God comes into your life and makes promises, you struggle with wondering how He will fulfill them? The Lord tells you, "I will bless you," and you look at yourself, your background, your education, and your bank account and ask, "How?" The Lord says, "I will take you out of this place, and you'll go somewhere else," and suddenly you struggle with how God is going to do it. You're not in doubt that He will do it, but you're concerned with *how* He will do it. Mary didn't know how Jesus would be born because she had not known a man.

God sometimes lays on you a powerful mission with details so strange and unique that it's impossible to share them with anyone. If Mary were to come into your church at age 14, engaged to Joseph, who is older, you would be talking about the age gap. If Mary were to start talking about being pregnant, the question would become "Who's the father?" Joseph says that he isn't the father. Then Mary says that she's pregnant with God. At what point would she be kicked out of the church?

But Mary had a cousin, Elizabeth, whom she could tell. Elizabeth was older and more experienced. The younger woman was given an unlikely miracle, and the older woman was also given an unlikely miracle (Luke 1:36–45). Elizabeth was pregnant and would deliver John the Baptist. As you can guess, they probably had long chats about the bearing of gifts that bring sorrow and pain. Mary's gift was given in a way that was unbearable and not approved by her culture.

Facing the Unbearable

Sometimes God can give you a glorious burden that is unbearable. What happens when you get to the point where you can no longer carry the burden? How can you face it? How should you face it? The following four truths can help you to face the unbearable.

1. God's plan is different from yours. Scripture says that Mary was engaged to Joseph and was ready to be married to him. There were wedding plans and goals for a new home, work, and starting a family. Then God came in with a different plan. Never lose the fact that God has a different plan from yours. You may pull it together. You may strategize. But if God wants to use you, He will interrupt your plan and use you the way He wants to use you.

Look through Scripture. Can you find anybody in Scripture who was ever used by God with his or her own plan? God uses people, not their plans. The dreamer Joseph was happy with his robe of many colors (Genesis 37:3), but God had a plan for him. No matter how great your plan seems to you, God sees much more than you could ever hope to see. Don't cease to plan and strategize, but you must understand that all your plans are tentative.

I've seen people work forty to fifty years, and when they walked into retirement, they were ready to buy a chair from Cracker Barrel and rock themselves into every sunset. But God had a different plan.

Some have waited a long time for children. Others prepare to be empty nesters as their children leave home. Some are thrilled at the thought of having grandchildren someday. But what if these things don't happen? What then?

Many people lose faith when God comes in and shuts things down, but He has a plan. Abraham left all he knew, the safety of a city where he was wealthy and popular, because God told him to move (Genesis 12). God had a different plan.

Saul, who became the apostle Paul, had a plan. He became famous for killing Christians all over the world. Then he traveled the Damascus Road, and God came in with a different plan (Acts 9).

What does this mean for you? You need to learn to believe the unlikely. If God is going to walk in your life, you need strength. Develop a muscle for believing the unlikely. The unexpected will happen, and if you've made yourself ready for God to move, it'll be easier.

2. God's plan will be more difficult than yours. As human beings, we're looking for the easiest route with the most gain in happiness. God has different plans, not necessarily to make you wealthy, but to make you better. Why are those plans so difficult? Because God's plans can be executed only by faith. Your plans are easy because they are in the human realm and usually involve things you know and see. God's plans are difficult because they are in the supernatural realm and have effects that you may never know.

Mary was confronted with this very issue. The angel told her that she was going to have a child. She had never even had relations with a man, but somehow she would have a child, and she was just supposed to go with it? The answer is yes. Have faith. It will be okay.

Paul said that "we walk by faith, not by sight" (2 Corinthians 5:7 ESV). God's plans are hard because you didn't make them; therefore, you don't know what will happen next. But when you see the things He has put together, it's amazing. Remember that you're working with Him. The joy is not in *what* you experience; the joy is in *who* gives you the experience.

God's plans may bring in trouble. Look at Mary. People believed that she was pregnant with an illegitimate child. People tend to think that when you are with God, everyone will love you, understand you, and cheer for you. But even after Christ had become a grown man, some people kept the rumor that Mary had slept with a man before marriage (John 8:41). Obeying God may bring unbearable rumors that affect your reputation.

God's plan will be more difficult than yours. Just ask Moses. His solution to the injustices against his people was to retaliate with murder. He ran for his life, but God sent him back to deliver the Israelites. He rose above the rumors about him and stepped into the role God had chosen for him.

It was evil for Potiphar's wife to accuse Joseph of something he didn't do. It was evil for his brothers to throw him into a pit. It was evil for him to be sold into slavery. Joseph went from being a cherished son to a slave with a life full of injustice, but God would raise him to the most powerful position in Egypt under Pharaoh.

3. God's plan will be better than yours. Gabriel told Mary that her son was going to be great. Was she thinking about His greatness as the troubles of the immediate future struck? When Herod tried to kill him? When she was ridiculed for having an illegitimate child? I doubt it. Did Joseph of the Old Testament think of the greatness that was about to strike as he rotted in a jail cell? No. They waited on God, who had a far better plan than just letting them out of their troubles. The trials were preparing them for incredible things.

I don't think that when Daniel and his friends went to Babylon (Daniel 1), he thought that he would someday be sitting in a lion's den (Daniel 6). Daniel decided that he was going to be faithful to God's plan because he believed that God's plan would be better. Not only did God preserve Daniel's life, He also used him for His purposes.

4. God's plan is more rewarding than yours. When it's all said and done, God's plan has better results than yours would. Can you imagine how Mary and Joseph are going to feel when we all are saved and in glory? All these people are saved because of their willingness to obey without explanations!

When you are going through the process, it is hard, but you can find encouragement in the plan of God. God says, "I know the plans I have for you, ... plans to prosper you and not to harm you, plans to give you hope and a future" (Jeremiah 29:11 NIV). It's not the plan that's the issue. It's the process of the plan that bothers us, the movement from Part A to Part B, with some pain and sacrifice involved.

You do some things not because you are happy to do them, but because you are with God. What does that mean? The journey of the Christian involves walking by faith, not by what we see. You're going to come across some things in your life that you wouldn't experience if you weren't walking with God. On your own, you're traveling a path that is simply survival. With God, your faith is a journey that will take you to many places where you never expected to go.

Many of us are not willing to go to the next level because we are looking for logic or reason before we respond with obedience. We want to know how or why. When you go for a surgery, you don't ask your doctor,

"What exactly are you going to do to my insides?" You have faith that the doctor knows best and will do what needs to be done. It isn't logical to cut a person open, but when someone is sick, slicing the person open is the illogical thing that may allow for healing. Sometimes you have to break something to fix it.

God's plan for your life will be more rewarding than anything you can come up with. You may be getting cut open, but that's because this season of your life is about true fixes, cutting you open to produce real healing.

Willingness

Many of us rob God of His glory because we talk about our lives and our plans as if we always know what our lives will become. You limit your praise factor when you think that you've got it all because you did it all. It didn't work that way. God worked your past to get you where you are in your present.

You limit your gratitude factor when you convince yourself and other people that it was you who orchestrated things, that you did everything and planned all this. Maybe you went to school for it. Okay, you just added some skills He could use. Maybe you avoided some bad places. Maybe your family is perfect. Great. If it were not for the plan of God on every one of our lives, you wouldn't have gotten all that. Not everyone has been away from bad places. Some grew up with bad families. Give God credit for the good things He continues to do in growing you up and training you for His use.

God's plan is better than mine. I'll listen to Jesus. I'm willing to do what He says. Willingness is about knowing whom and what you're following. You're willing yourself not to follow Satan and instead to follow Jesus.

Judas had the best pastor in the world, and his pastor's name was Jesus. Judas had a pastor who could work miracles, yet he became the most famous traitor ever. He was willing to follow Satan instead of Jesus.

Lucifer served directly under God in heaven. Lucifer stood by the throne and was unwilling to bow before God. He had direct access to God, and he is a demon today. Do you know what the difference was? Willingness.

You are where you are because of your willingness. When the doctor gives you a prescription, are you willing to take it? Do you have a prescription you aren't taking because you're not willing to stick with the program? If that's the case, your life may be in danger. You are where you are because of your unwillingness. If you don't take the medicine, you will have to pay the consequences.

There is no magic to it. Are you willing to stay the course? Are you willing to hold your feet to the fire? Are you willing to trust Him in the unbearable? When nothing makes sense, when everything confuses you, where is your willingness?

It's time to update your willingness. Sometimes when I'm looking at my iPad, a message comes up saying that there's new software. I have to give my permission to update it. I have to be willing. If I'm not willing, my iPad will not function at its full capacity.

If you are willing to let God work on you, if you are willing to trust in His plan, then you are in for great rewards. True healing and God's blessings will come as you become the person He intends you to be. It's time to update your spiritual software and follow God's plan!

WORKBOOK

Chapter Seven Questions

Question: Describe a blessing God has given you that is also a burden. What are some things about this blessing and burden that are so unique that they are hard for others to understand? What should you do when you face others' judgment or assumptions about what God is doing in your life?

_____

_____

_____

_____

_____

_____

_____

_____

_____

_____

Question: Do praise and gratitude characterize your life, or do you take the credit for who you have become and the good things that have happened to you? Do you pride yourself on being self-made, or do you see yourself as a willing participant in God's story?

Journal: What has surprised you along the way about how God's plans for you have been different and more difficult, yet also better and more rewarding than your own plans?

Action: Read a biography or memoir of someone who was greatly used by God. Note the ways God's plans for this person were different from his or her own plans. What difficulties did this person face? How were God's plans better and more rewarding than what he or she ever imagined?

Chapter Seven Notes

CHAPTER EIGHT

Thriving in the Unbearable

Remember the story from the previous chapter? An angel visited Mary to tell her that she would have a child. She wondered how, since she wasn't married and was a virgin. The angel told her how it would work.

> *The angel answered, "The Holy Spirit will come on you, and the power of the Most High will overshadow you. So the holy one to be born will be called the Son of God. Even Elizabeth your relative is going to have a child in her old age, and she who was said to be unable to conceive is in her sixth month. For no word from God will ever fail."*
>
> *"I am the Lord's servant," Mary answered. "May your word to me be fulfilled." Then the angel left her.*
> —**Luke 1:35–38** *(NIV)*

This is a familiar story. Perhaps you know the story so well that you have missed or forgotten some of its powerful lessons. Mary wasn't just to be the mother of God and receive all the blessings that come with that position. She had to endure the unbearable. Still, she thrived. How?

Joseph and Mary were engaged to be married. Mary

had her life mapped out, and in one moment, God told her through an angel that her life was about to change. Life can change in a moment. We all experience that. Sometimes God sends messengers in the shape of doctors who tell you that you have a disease, like cancer. Sometimes your car breaks down and you don't have the money to pay the bill. You may get a surprise pregnancy, like Mary, or you may lose a loved one. How do you endure? How can you thrive in the unbearable?

There Are People Who Need You

Is God throwing you into a place where you cannot identify with anyone? Are you all alone in your trouble? The answer is no! When God calls you to do something that you have never done, you may attack the people around you. In Mary's case, that's why the angel told Mary about Elizabeth (Luke 1:36). How did Elizabeth fit in with Mary's story? The angel was giving her someone to relate to. What Mary was about to face was huge, and she had no clue about what to do, but she didn't have to go through it alone.

Get a support system. Find someone in your family or a close friend, someone who is older and wiser, and connect with that person. God has given you a glorious burden, a gift few have ever had, something that most cannot relate to. There is no formula for it.

Elizabeth was there when Mary needed her. They were going through similar things, though not the same thing. You need to connect with others in similar circumstances so you can help each other.

How Do I Thrive?

God will always orchestrate events in your life. If it is God's will, it will be God's bill. That means He has the restaurant ticket. He will take care of you. Whatever God allows to come your way, He is the author of it. God is the one who sustains, maintains, and affirms. He is the best one to do this because He is in charge of the whole affair.

When God comes into your life, He is not coming to interrupt your life. No, God doesn't interrupt your life. He always comes to intervene in your life. He is helping, saving you from something far worse. When God intervenes in your life, it's a God moment.

Read through Scripture and you will find men and women who had God moments. When Moses was minding his business, he had a God moment with the burning bush (Exodus 3:1–4:17). Joseph had a God moment as he interpreted dreams (Genesis 40–41). When God originates it, He is going to orchestrate it.

After the burning bush, Moses moved back to Egypt to free God's people. After interpreting the dreams, Joseph rose quickly to become ruler over Egypt. When God gives you a God moment, it will always give birth to a God movement. As you wait on God for whatever He has told you to wait for, whatever burden He has put on your heart, whatever blessing He has put on your path, learn that one moment with God creates movement.

Many things revolve around a conversation. Adam and Eve were minding their own business when a serpent talked from the tree. They talked and listened, and they lost everything (Genesis 3). They acted on what they heard in the conversation.

When God wants to do something amazing in your life or if you're being tempted to do evil, you need to watch out for the surrounding conversation. Not all talk is just talk. The Bible says, "Death and life are in the power of the tongue…" (Proverbs 18:21 ESV). Every word will bring either success or loss in your life and with those around you. There is no empty conversation. Every conversation will bear some fruit, whether good or bad. You thrive on these conversations, or you sink yourself, so watch your conversations.

How Do You See Yourself?

Mary was just a simple village girl, and she was young. She didn't know much. She was an underdog. Her parents and her pedigree are not spoken of in the Bible. It seems there was nothing about her that was special. She was just Mary. She wasn't even the only one called Mary. There are a lot of Marys in the Bible. She was so ordinary, yet our extraordinary God hand-picked her for an extraordinary assignment. God is attracted to ordinary people. Why? Because He changes us for extraordinary assignments.

The way you think about yourself must change. When God chooses you for an assignment, it's for a reason. Are you thinking that you're something? Not really. You're nothing. God may have to take you down a few notches. Do you think that you're nothing? Good. God is ready to build you. Gabriel told Mary that she was "highly favored" (Luke 1:28 NIV). Wow. She was just an ordinary person, yet she was highly favored by God.

In the Bible, Mary was not the only one God raised. When Gideon was feeling blue, an angel came in and said, "The LORD is with you, O mighty man of valor" (Judges 6:12 ESV). Gideon wondered, "Why me?" Who was he, really? His clan was the smallest, and he was the runt of the litter (Judges 6:15). He was the coward of all cowards, but God said, "I didn't make a mistake. You're chosen, Gideon." And you are chosen as well.

When God changes you, the way you think about yourself must change. Why? For you to be exceptional, you need to be at peace with being the exception. You'll stand out and be different, and that's okay. Embrace it.

Whenever you are different, the first thing that people

do is grow suspicious. Then they talk about you. Are you strong enough to handle it? Or, more accurately, is your thinking in the right place so you can continue to be the person God means for you to be? After your trials, you're going to be the person God means for you to be, and you're going to stand out.

You may have a calling that requires you to find those who can relate to you. That was Mary. With whom would she share her news? The only person she told her story to, according to Scripture, was Elizabeth. Two women with divine assignments were interrupted by their calling. They connected on a level that no one else in the world would understand. They both had to adjust their thinking.

You must hang around folks who believe in miracles. When Mary arrived at Elizabeth's house and greeted her, the baby in Elizabeth leapt in excitement at being close to Christ (Luke 1:39–45). You need to be around people who make your "baby" leap, figuratively speaking. Whatever God has said will leap up.

Most people's hearts don't leap when they come across your calling. Instead, they want to crush it. They think that you're lying about it. You are captivated by your calling, but God occasionally gives you people who will let you know that you're not alone. They will help you to change your mindset from having many friends on a superficial level to having only a few close friends.

Discipline

God has asked you to wait during the unbearable, all while carrying something you've never seen before, a promise from God. It takes discipline.

Submit to God's discipline. Joseph was tempted with Potiphar's wife and had to be a disciplined brother not to mess up the story God was writing for him. It's not that God didn't have a blessing with Joseph's name on it; He did. But the question was: How bad did Joseph want God's blessing?

How disciplined are you? The issue is not whether or not your mistakes could blow up your career. That's not in your hands. You must deal with how disciplined you are—that's the only part in your control. The issue is not that you won't get the college degree. The question is how disciplined you are.

Mary's fiancé, Joseph, had his own dreams of a wife and a family, but God had a dream of saving humanity. Mary and Joseph, at the same time, had to learn to align their dreams with God's dream. When frustrations come, God still wants you to achieve His goals. You need to align your goals with God's goals. How did Mary and Joseph connect? They aligned goals. Joseph steered his will toward Mary's, and they made it work. This will work only if you align your goals with God's.

What to Do While You Wait

How does God use my circumstance to get me ready for the future? What am I to do when God is positioning me and preparing me for Him to accomplish His vision for my life? Mary asked the same question of the angel: "How will this be...?" (Luke 1:34 ESV). How is this going to happen, and what can I do to make it come about?

Remember Mary's cousin and friend, Elizabeth? Her husband, Zechariah, was going through a journey similar to Joseph's (Luke 1:5–25). He and Elizabeth were old when an angel told him that he was going to be a father. He doubted because they were so old. The angel sealed his mouth in punishment for his doubt. The first time he would be allowed to speak again was when he named the child. Instead of people saying that Elizabeth was pregnant, people were coming to check on the priest who could not speak.

For nine months, Zechariah understood that his limitations were not a punishment; they were confirmation that God was working in the family. Elizabeth was in the house, wondering if things were really going to work out, and all she needed was her husband's lack of voice as confirmation that God was working.

What had seemed bad, losing the voice, was a reminder that God was working. If your faith becomes shaky while you wait on God, look for His work, and you'll be reminded that He is still there.

Embrace Divine Hook-ups

Divine hook-ups are the friendships God brings into your life when you need them. Elizabeth, an old woman, was six months pregnant, and she needed someone to connect with as much as Mary did.

The power of associations is an important thing whenever God wants to do something with your life. The saying that "birds of a feather flock together" is true. Find someone who can believe just as you do. Mary had to believe that this Holy Spirit child was God's child. Elizabeth had to believe that, even in her old age, she was pregnant with a missionary child who was to introduce Mary's child. Elizabeth's child would be John the Baptist. Their burden for their calling brought them together, and they encouraged each other to submit to God's plan.

There is something about associations that is a gift from God. Think of David and Jonathan in the Bible. David was struggling to survive while the king, Saul, tried to kill him. Saul's son, Jonathan, grew close to David (1 Samuel 18:1–4). That association carried David through many challenging times, and they both became better men because of their friendship. There was no one else who would understand where David was in life. That friendship was invaluable.

The opposite of these positive associations is *separation*. Some people won't understand that God has given you a unique calling. This will make people uncomfortable with you. It will separate those who will not help you from the ones God has given you as divine hook-ups.

Find someone going through similar circumstances whose fire is brighter than yours. This will help you to thrive through the unbearable and bring you into closer alignment with what God has for you.

WORKBOOK

Chapter Eight Questions

Question: Who is your support group (or support person)? How have they helped you to walk through this season of waiting? How can you be that person for someone else?

_____
_____
_____
_____
_____
_____
_____
_____
_____
_____
_____
_____

Question: What discipline is needed in your life as you wait on God? How can you remain motivated to be disciplined when you are tempted, tired, or discouraged from a long season of waiting?

_____
_____
_____
_____
_____
_____
_____
_____
_____
_____

Journal: Recall the clearest God moments in your life. How has each led to a God movement?

_____
_____
_____
_____
_____
_____

_____

_____

_____

_____

_____

Action: Take time to thank the person who has been an "Elizabeth" in your life. If you do not have an encourager like that, ask God to bring such a relationship into your life, someone uniquely equipped to understand your situation and to help you stay focused on God and His plan for you.

Chapter Eight Notes

CONCLUSION

Bust a Move

Do you remember our opening Scriptures? Hannah was going to have a child. She named the boy Samuel and gave him to the Lord (1 Samuel 1:20–28). Samuel served in the temple. In fact, he grew close to Eli, the priest who had thought Hannah was drunk (1 Samuel 2:11).

> *The boy Samuel ministered before the LORD under Eli. In those days the word of the LORD was rare; there were not many visions.*
>
> *One night Eli, whose eyes were becoming so weak that he could barely see, was lying down in his usual place. The lamp of God had not yet gone out, and Samuel was lying down in the house of the LORD, where the ark of God was. Then the LORD called Samuel.*
>
> *Samuel answered, "Here I am." And he ran to Eli and said, "Here I am; you called me."*
>
> *But Eli said, "I did not call; go back and lie down." So he went and lay down.*
>
> *Again the LORD called, "Samuel!" And Samuel got up and went to Eli and said, "Here I am; you called me."*

> "My son," Eli said, "I did not call; go back and lie down."
>
> Now Samuel did not yet know the Lord: The word of the Lord had not yet been revealed to him.
>
> A third time the Lord called, "Samuel!" And Samuel got up and went to Eli and said, "Here I am; you called me."
>
> Then Eli realized that the Lord was calling the boy. So Eli told Samuel, "Go and lie down, and if he calls you, say, 'Speak, Lord, for your servant is listening.'" So Samuel went and lay down in his place.
>
> The Lord came and stood there, calling as at the other times, "Samuel! Samuel!"
>
> Then Samuel said, "Speak, for your servant is listening."
> —*1 Samuel 3:1-10* (NIV)

Samuel didn't know the Lord yet, but now God was going to reveal Himself to Samuel. Notice what Samuel was doing before God spoke to him. He was serving the Lord. He ministered before the Lord.

Have You Heard from God?

Like Samuel, you can be faithful in something you don't know and still be working for God. Sometimes it is your shortcomings that position you for God to reveal Himself. Let's banish this idea of spiritual heroes. Let's do away with them. Away with those who can explain God to all of us! Away with those who try to define God and put Him in a box! You can serve God and not know a thing about Him.

What do I mean? You may not be doing things in the church and the community because you think that you are not Christian enough. Stop being impressed by people. Celebrate grace. If anybody does right, celebrate God.

Don't make that person a hero; just praise God.

It all revolves around God's grace helping you. If it weren't for grace, I would not be writing this book. If you have questioned your walk with God, wondering if God really approves of you and is pleased with you, you need to hear this. There are moments when I feel like quitting. There are moments when it looks like it doesn't make any sense to keep going and I've not heard a word from God.

Perhaps you came to church all year long. You were in the choir. You were an usher. You were a deacon. You even taught others. But deep down in your heart, you felt empty. You told everybody about how good God is, yet you were questioning if that was real in your life. I've discovered that my best sermons were when I was at my worst, when I wasn't hearing from God and I felt awful.

When You Miss the Voice

The word of the Lord came to Samuel, and he didn't catch it. Are you afraid that you'll miss His voice? Guess what, He is calling again. He is not going to give you a chance not to hear.

When Samuel heard the voice, he went and got advice from Eli. Eli told him to tell the voice that he was listening. Are you in a situation where you're not sure what to do next, where you're painfully broken and still waiting? Your situation is going to give you a revelation of God's grace. Whatever your situation is, it is good enough to give you special access to God's insight. Every experience is your teacher. Every situation is setting you up to get a revelation from God. You've got to listen and then tell Him that you're ready.

Your Commitment Is More Important Than Your Mistakes

God is willing to go to great lengths to drive you out of your average way of thinking. Average is the village you're in. Your village is the normal. It's what you're used to, but God doesn't want you there. Samuel was being called because he was in a comfortable place, and he was not going to budge unless God gave him a little shove.

Samuel went to his village to get feedback on the new voice. He went to the safe place. But his purpose was more valuable than his mistakes. He had a mission, and God wasn't going to let him go.

When God wants to elevate you above your village and the village mentality, don't resist. There are many who are not growing in their spiritual walks because they believe that God won't talk to them. They think that their mistakes are too big or too many, so they turn away when His voice arrives. That's simply not how God works. God speaks for a reason. He speaks, and things happen. He is not going to avoid you because you've made some mistakes.

God didn't stop calling out to Samuel. He called again and again. He didn't give up on Samuel, and Samuel finally answered.

Why doesn't God give up on us? Because God's grace is more powerful than your ignorance, your stupidity, and even your death. How many times have you looked at yourself and called yourself dumb? God's grace is so powerful that it is the only thing willing to come and chill with you in your foolishness, no matter what you say about yourself, and leave you with dignity.

First John 4:19 says, "We love Him because He first loved us" (NKJV). All of us are awful people, and He still loved us first. When you look around and discover that He is there, you can respond in kind.

Once He has got you, He is going to mature you. Don't

fight the process. Learn to expect God to mature you. The process may mean calling you four times before you finally get it. The process may mean that you get up three times, run to another room, and make a fool of yourself in front of others. Why not answer the first time? If God keeps calling you, keep on answering. The process matures you, and God is more concerned about your maturity than simply getting things done.

You will always believe God in proportion to your view of God. When your view of God is huge, you will discover your ability to show humility. Humility is determined by the size of God that you have in your mind and heart. If He is a small God to you, there is no way you can be humble because your ego is too big, making you godlike in your own view. But when you understand that He is a big God, you will discover that it is easy for you to take your place. When God has an assignment for you and wants to use you, the work ahead will be less painful.

As your view of God gets higher, you will discover that your appetite for certain things goes away. Sin melts away because the appeal is gone. Some people look sinless because they simply have no appetite for sin.

Pray that God will help to upgrade your view of Him. Say, as Samuel did, "Speak, for your servant is listening" (1 Samuel 3:10 NIV). You're the servant, and God is the master.

Bust That Move!

The rich man Zacchaeus was up in a tree because he was determined to catch a glimpse of Jesus, but he was too short to see in the crowd (Luke 19:1–4). Jesus came to the tree and gave Zacchaeus an opportunity (Luke 19:5). Not only did Zacchaeus see Jesus, but the tax collector was so impressed that it changed his life. Zacchaeus said, "Look, Lord! Here and now I give half of my possessions to the poor, and if I have cheated anybody out of anything, I will pay back four times the amount" (Luke 19:8 NIV). He was saying, "I'm going to bust a move."

Busting a move is when God gives you an opportunity to do right and you take it. You've learned, you've been through it, and it's time to bust a move. Samuel missed it three times, but the fourth time he busted a move. He called out to God, and it changed his life. God is always giving opportunities.

Do you know the difference between David and Saul? Saul was mad in jealousy because he missed his opportunity. Saul was mad at David because David took his opportunity in the face of adversity and Saul didn't (1 Samuel 17–18). The same thing is true in the church. Most people who are mad at you missed their shot. You haven't done anything wrong. They just wish that they were standing where you are standing. They had the opportunity, and they didn't use it. It was you who busted a move at the right time. Older people who are happy are the ones who enjoyed their opportunities throughout life.

The wrong things you've done and repented of are burned like hay in a fire. If you focus instead on the right that you didn't do, you're going to discover that possibilities and hope will enter because whatever you focus on changes the results. If you focus on the wrong that you've done, it's going to impact your results. If you focus on the right you haven't done, all hope is not lost because you'll try to do those right things in the present. Samuel himself, one of the world's greatest prophets, missed three calls by the almighty God before he got it right.

God has been speaking to you. You might not have done what you're supposed to do or gone where you're supposed to go, but all hope is not lost. Now is the time to start down the path toward right, which is the path toward God. In your time of waiting, your time of training, you can find success, God, and yourself.

Don't forget to bust a move when you hear God calling. Turn to Him and cry, "Speak! Your servant is listening!"

About the Author

Pastor Mackenzie Kambizi holds many titles: visionary shepherd, agent of compassion, theological ethicist, biblical expositor, revivalist, evangelist, conference speaker, congregational transformer, community developer, cultural critic, folklorist, and dramatist. He works from a practical, relevant, and biblical approach when teaching Scripture. His personal philosophy is *Bad News Won't Change My Mind*!

Pastor Mackenzie Kambizi is a family man blessed with three elegant ladies—Madison, Morgan, and Unathi—and a handsome son, Mackenzie Jr. As a family, they believe that together they must champion the kingdom of God till the last trump sounds—PushTheKingdom!

REFERENCES

Notes

[1] Chambers, Oswald. *My Utmost for His Highest.* Updated language. Our Daily Bread Publishing, 2010.

www.ingramcontent.com/pod-product-compliance
Lightning Source LLC
Chambersburg PA
CBHW070204100426
42743CB00013B/3035